Introductory Stories for Reproduction 2

L. A. Hill

Oxford University Press
外 國 語 研 修 社

Oxford University Press

Oxford London Glasgow
New York Toronto Melbourne Auckland
Kuala Lumpur Singapore Hong Kong Tokyo
Delhi Bombay Calcutta Madras Karachi
Nairobi Dar Es Salaam Cape Town

and associates in
Beirut Berlin Ibadan Mexico City Nicosia

© Oxford University Press (Tokyo) 1982

First Korean impression 1985

ISBN 0 19 589094 9 (East Asian Edition)
ISBN 0 19 589096 5 (UK Edition)

Illustrated by Dennis Mallet

Printed in Korea

영어의 표현력 및 이해력 양성에 역점을 둔 L.A.HILL 박사의
명저 Stories for Reproduction 총서 한국판을 내놓으면서

우리의 국력이 크게 신장되어 국제 교류의 폭이 확대되어 감에 따라 각계 각층에서 영어에 능통한 인재의 요구가 날로 늘어가고 있습니다. 그러나 이러한 실력을 갖춘 인재는 구하기가 쉽지 않을 뿐 아니라, 최고 학부를 나온 분들 마저 영어를 필요로 하는 업무에 부닥치면 표현력(말과 글로 표현하기)이나 이해력(읽거나 듣고 이해하기) 부족 때문에 많은 곤란을 겪고 있습니다.

따지고 보면 이러한 현상이 생기게 된 것은 당연한 결과라고 할 수 있겠습니다. 왜냐하면 지금까지의 영어 교육이 난해한 영문의 국역이나 까다로운 문법체계의 학습에 치중한 나머지 작문력, 회화력, 독해력 특히 속독력 및 청해력 등을 양성하는 학습을 소홀히 해 왔기 때문입니다.

그렇다면 영어의 표현력과 이해력을 기르기 위해서는 무엇부터 시작하여 어떻게 해야 하는지 그 구체적인 방법을 살펴 보기로 합시다.

1. 상용 2000 단어의 철저한 학습과 활용

영어로 일상적인 의사표시를 하는 데 있어서는 빈도수가 높은 것만을 뽑아 만든 2,000 상용 단어만의 사용으로 부족함이 없습니다. 예를 들면 6만의 표제어와 6만 9천의 예문을 싣고 있는 Longman Dictionary of Contemporary English는 표제어의 정의와 그 예문을 제시하는 데 2,000의 「정의 어휘(Defining Vocabulary)」와 단순한 문법구조만을 쓰고 있으며, Longman Dictionary of Business English도 Michael West의 상용 영어 단어 일람표(A General Service List of English Words)를 토대로 한 2,000여 단어와 단순한 문법구조만으로 Business 각 분야의 전문용어를 완벽하게 해설하고 있습니다.

이런 사실만을 보아도 영어 실력 양성에 있어서 2,000 상용 단어의 철저한 학습과 그 활용연습이 얼마나 중요한 것이라는 것을 쉽게 이해할 수 있을 것입니다.

그럼에도 불구하고 이 2,000 상용 단어의 철저한 기초학습이 채 끝나기도 전에, 일상적 의사표시에는 별로 쓰이지 않아 기억하기도 힘든 많은 어려운 영어 단어들(고교 수준에서는 약 5,000, 대학과 대학원 수준에서는 10,000~30,000단어)을 단편적, 기계적으로 암기하거나 난해한 영문의 국역이나 까다로운 문법체계의 학습에만 매달린다면 아무리 노력을 해 봤자 모래 위에 성을 쌓는 격이어서, 영어로 자신의 생각을 자유롭게 표현할 수 있는 정도까지 그 실력이 향상되기를 기대할 수 없는 것입니다.

2. 문맥적 접근법(Contextualized Approach)

어학의 습득은 「의미내용」의 「기억, 재현」과정을 통해 이루어지는 것이며, 이 「의미내용」을 전달하는 효율은 1. 숫자(Figure) 2. 문자(Letter) 3. 단어(Word) 4. 문(Sentence) 5. 문장의 절(Paragraph)순으로, 그것이 함축하는 「의미내용」의 차원이 높은 것일수록 그 전달량이 커지고 전달 효율이 높아집니다. 따라서 영어 학습에 있어서도 단어나 문법을 따로 학습하는 것보다는 문장내에서 문맥(Context)에 따라 이를 학습하는 것이 그 기억과 재현의 효율을 높일 수 있는 것입니다.

3. 표현력 향상을 위한 재현(Reproduction)연습

영어의 표현력을 기르는 데는 모범적인 영어 문장을 되풀이해서 읽고 이것을 재현(Reproduction)하는 연습을 해 보는 것이 가장 효과적이라는 것은 이미 널리 알려진 사실입니다. 그래서 중·고교의 교과서를 한 권이라도 암기해 보라고 권유하는 분들이 많으나, 이 교과서 자체가 암기와 재현 연습용으로 쓰기에는, 본문의 길이가 너무 길거나 난해할 뿐 아니라 재현 연습을 유도하는 적절한 Questions, Exercises 및 Answer Key 등의 뒷받침이 되어 있지 않기 때문에 표현력 향상을 위한 교재로는 적합하지 못합니다.

영어 교육계의 오랜 경험에서 밝혀진 바에 의하면 표현력 양성을 목적으로 하는 영어 문장 재현 연습용의 교재는 다음과 같은 요건을 갖춘 것이 가장 효과가 높다는 것입니다.

첫째 교재 본문의 내용이 학습자의 지속적인 흥미와 관심을 끌 수 있을 만큼 재미 있으면서도 교육적 가치가 풍부한 것이어야 하며,

둘째 교재에 사용되는 단어, 숙어, 문법구조등이 각 학습단계(입문, 초급, 중급, 상급수준 등)에 꼭 알맞게 제한 사용되어야 하며,

셋째 재현 연습에 쓰일 본문의 길이도 기억과 재현에 알맞는 단어수(학습 단계에 따라 150 단어 내지 350 단어의 길이)를 초과하지 않아야 하고,

넷째 학습시키고자 하는 단어, 숙어, 문법구조등이 교재의 본문에 흡수·통합되어 이것들이 각기 따로 따로 유리되어 있을 때 보다 높은 차원의 「의미내용」을 갖도록 하여야 한다는 것입니다.

따라서 영어의 표현력과 이해력의 종합적인 향상을 위해서는 무엇보다 먼저 위에 열거한 네가지 요건을 갖춘 교재가 절대 필요한 것입니다. 그런데 이러한 교재의 입수가 지극히 어렵던 차에, 다행히 옥스포드대학출판부에서, 이 방면의 세계적 권위자인 L.A. HILL 박사로 하여금 위에 적은 네가지 요건을 모두 갖춘 영어 학습교재 총서를 저술케하여, 이를 최근에 모두 펴 내놓아 외국어로서 영어를 배우는 전세계 영어학도들의 절

찬을 받고 있는 것을 보고, 실용 영어의 통신교육과 그에 부수되는 영어 교재의 **출판**을 전문으로 하고 있는 저희 外國語研修社에서는, 이 교재의 한국내 출판이 저희들의 사업목적에 부합될 뿐 아니라 이러한 교재를 찾고 있는 수 많은 독자와 영어 교사들에게 크게 도움이 되리라고 생각하고 작년부터 옥스포드대학출판부와 판권 교섭을 해 오던 끝에 금년들어 계약이 성립되어 L. A. HILL 박사 저술의 영어 학습 교재중 **표현력** 및 이해력 향상에 역점을 둔 교재 전 **4**집을 아래와 같이 내놓게 되었읍니다.

제1집 **Stories for Reproduction 1**: 입문편, 초급편, 중급편 및 상급편의 Text 각 1권과 그 Study Guide(학습안내서)각 1권 및 이에 딸린 음성교재용 녹음테이프.

제2집 **Stories for Reproduction 2**: 입문편, 초급편, 중급편 및 상급편의 Text 각 1권과 그 Answer Key 각 1권 및 이에 딸린 음성교재용 녹음테이프.

제3집 **Steps to Understanding**: 입문편, 초급편, 중급편 및 상급편의 Text 각 1권과 그 Answer Key 각 1권 및 이에 딸린 음성교재용 녹음테이프.

제4집 **Stories for Reproduction (American Series)** : 초급편, 중급편 및 상급편의 Text 각 1권과 그 **Answer Key** 및 이에 딸린 음성교재용 녹음테이프.

전 세계적인 Best Seller 가 되어 있는 이 교재는 표현력과 독해력 향상에 필수적인 단어·숙어와 문법구조를 4단계로 나누어 제한 사용하고 있어 독자들에게 학습상의 부담을 주지 않을 뿐 아니라 그 본문이 유우머(해학)와 윗트(기지)로 가득찬 흥미진진한 짧은 이야기로 되어 있기 때문에 그것을 끝까지 단숨에 읽을 수 있도록 되어 있으며, 이 이야기를 속독, 청취, 정독, 재청(再聽)한 다음 다양한 **Questions**와 **Exercises** 를 사용한 문답식 방법으로 그 내용을 이해하는 훈련을 쌓는 동시에 이를 다시 말과 글로 표현해 보는(**Oral & Written Reproduction**)연습을 되풀이 함으로써, 난해한 영문국역, 단편적인 단어·숙어의 암기나 문법체계의 학습등에서 오는 정신적 긴장과 피로를 수반하지 않고, 독자들이 이야기의 내용을 즐기다 보면 자기도 모르는 사이에 이해력과 표현력이 몸에 붙도록 꾸며져 있읍니다.

또한 이 교재는 Text와는 따로 **Study Guide**(학습안내서), **Answer Key** (해답집) 및 녹음테이프가 딸려 있어 개인의 자습(Self-Study)용으로는 물론 교실 수업용으로도 쓸 수 있도록 만들어져 있읍니다.

이 교재가 많은 독자들의 영어 표현력 및 이해력 향상에 획기적인 도움이 되기를 바랍니다.

1985년 1월 5일

外國語研修社

代表理事
會 長　李 瀅 載

머 리 말

이 책은 흥미진진하면서도 평이한 이야기를 읽거나 듣고 그 내용을 기억하여 자신의 말과 글로 되도록 많이 재표현해 봄으로써 영어의 이해력(讀解・聽解)과 표현력 (作文・會話)을 향상시킬 목적으로 쓰여진 Stories for Reproduction Series 2 (이야기의 재현을 통해 배우는 영어 총서 제 2 집)의 입문편입니다.

이 책에는 모두 30편의 이야기가 담겨 있으며, 그 길이는 각각 150단어 정도이고 이야기마다 그 내용에 대한 질의문(Questions)과 그 활용을 위한 연습문제(Exercises)가 뒤따르고 있습니다. 이 책은 L. A. Hill 박사의 750표제어 수준으로 쓰여져 있으며 그 어휘는 권말의 부록에 수록되어 있습니다. 이야기들 중에는 750표제어 수준을 넘는 단어 한 두개를 포함한 것도 약간 있으나 이 단어들은 그 이야기가 실린 페이지의 아랫쪽에 주석이 되어 있습니다. 또한 연습문제의 지시문에 Space, Choose, Mean(v), Puzzle (n), Opposite(n), Sentence(n), Story등 몇 개의 단어가 나오는데 이것들은 선생님이 가르쳐 주시거나 사전을 찾아 보시면 될 것 입니다. 그리고 문법구조는 입문편에 알맞도록 엄격하게 통제되어 있습니다.

L. A. Hill 박사가 이책과 같은 수준(입문편)으로 쓴 책들은 다음과 같습니다.

Introductory Stories for Reproduction, Series 1

Introductory Steps to Understanding

A Second Reading Book

A Third Reading Book

Oxford Graded Readers, 750-Headword level : Junior and Senior Stories

이 책을 이용하는 방법

이 책에는 카셋트가 딸려 있어 혼자서 공부하는 학생들은 다음 (i) 및 (ii)의 방법으로 그것을 이용할 수 있습니다.

(i) 강세, 리듬, 억양을 포함한 발음연습

각자의 뜻대로 책을 펴거나 덮고 카셋트를 1 회 또는 그 이상 듣고 난 후 이야기를 소리내어 읽어 봅니다. 처음에는 카셋트를 따라서 읽고 다음에는 혼자서 읽어 봅니다. 혼자서 읽고 난 후에는 카셋트를 다시 들어 보고 잘못된 것(발음, 강세, 리듬 및 억양 등)을 바로잡습니다.

(ii) 청해(聽解 – 듣고 이해하기) 연습

책을 덮고 카셋트를 1 회 또는 그 이상 들은 다음 기억할 수 있는 **최대한도로** 이야기를 써 보고 / 써 보거나, 이야기를 보지 않고 질의문에 답하고 연습문제를 풀어 봅니다. 기억할 수 있는 최대한으로 이야기를 썼으면 자신이 쓴 것과 원문을 비교하기 위하여 책을 보거나 카셋트를 다시 들어 봐도 좋습니다.

(i)의 방법은 **강세, 리듬 및 억양**을 포함하여 정확한 **발음**을 익히는 연습을 시키는 것이 목적이며,

(ii)의 방법은 **청해력**(**聽解力** – 듣고 이해하기) 향상을 위한 연습을 시키는 것이 목적입니다.

혼자서 자력으로 공부하는 학생은 이 밖에 다음과 같은 (iii)의 방법을 사용할 수도 있겠습니다.

(iii) 독해(**讀解** – 읽고 이해하기) 연습

이야기를 음독(**音讀**) 또는 묵독(**黙讀**)으로 1 회 또는 그 이상 읽은 다음 기억할 수 있는 최대한 공책에 써 보고 / 써 보거나, 다시 이야기를 보지 말고 질의문에 답하고 연습문제를 풀어 봅니다. 이야기를 기억해서 최대한으로 써 본 다음에는 책에 쓰여진 이야기와 그것을 대조해 보고 잘못된 것을 바로잡습니다.

(iii)의 방법에 따른 공부는 독해(**讀解** – 읽고 이해하기)의 연습이 됩니다.

(ii) 와 (iii) 의 방법으로 공부하는 경우 이야기를 듣거나 읽는 것과 그것을 최대한으로 기억하여 재현(**再現**)하는 연습 사이에는 일정한 간격 – 며칠간 까지도 무방함 – 을 두어도 좋습니다.

이 책과는 별도로 연습문제에 대한 모범답안을 실은 교사용의 소책자 **Answer Key** 가 마련되어 있습니다.

Introduction

This is a new Introductory book to *Stories for Reproduction, Series 2*. Each story is about 150 words long and has questions and exercises after it. This book is written at Dr. L. A. Hill's 750-headword level. The vocabulary is given in the Appendix to this book. Some of the stories contain a few words outside this vocabulary; these are glossed on the pages on which they appear. There are also a few extra vocabulary items in the instructions to the exercises. These are *space, choose, mean (v.), opposite (n.), puzzle (n.), sentence (n.),* and *story.* The teacher can explain these words to the students, or ask them to look them up in a dictionary. The grammatical structures are also strictly graded.

Other books by Dr. Hill at this same level are:
Introductory Stories for Reproduction, Series 1
Introductory Steps to Understanding
A Second Reading Book
A Third Reading Book
Oxford Graded Readers, 750-headword level: Junior and Senior Stories

How to use this book:
There is a cassette of this book which the student working on his own can use in the following ways (i) and (ii):

(i) He can listen to the cassette one or more times (with his book open or closed, as he wishes) and then read the story aloud himself, at first in chorus with the voice on the cassette, and then alone. After his own reading alone, he can check his performance by listening to the cassette again.

(ii) He can listen to the cassette one or more times, with his book closed, and then write down as much of the story as he can remember, and/or answer the questions and do the exercises (all without looking at the story). If he writes as much of the story as he can remember, he can then look at the story in the book, or listen to it again on the cassette, to compare what he has written with the original.

(i) gives practice in speaking with a good pronunciation, including stress, rhythm and intonation.

(ii) gives practice in aural comprehension (listening and understanding).
In addition, the student working on his own can do (iii):

(iii) He can read the story to himself, aloud or silently, once or more than once, and then write down as much of the story as he can remember, and/or answer the questions and do the exercises, all without looking at the story again. If he writes as much of the story as he can remember, he can check his work afterwards by comparing it with the story in the book.

(iii) gives practice in reading comprehension (reading and understanding).

With (ii) and (iii) there can be an interval—even of several days— between the hearing or reading of the story and the reproduction (writing down as much as one can remember).

A separate Teacher's Booklet is available, containing model answers to the exercises.

Introductory Stories for Reproduction 2

1

Mrs. Jones wanted a picture for her living-room. She took the bus and went to town. She looked for a picture shop, and after a few minutes she found one. There were some pictures in the window, but she did not like them very much.

She went into the shop and looked at some other pictures. She liked some of those more. There was a picture of a young girl, and Mrs. Jones liked it very much. She went to the shopkeeper and said, 'How much do you want for this picture?'

The shopkeeper turned the picture round. He looked at the back of it and then said, 'Thirteen pounds.'

'Thirty pounds?' Mrs. Jones said. 'That's very expensive. I'm going to offer you twenty pounds for it.'

'I said, "Thirteen pounds", not "Thirty pounds",' the man answered.

'Thirteen?' Mrs. Jones said. 'Then I'm going to offer you nine pounds for it.'

Words not in the 750: offer (v.), shopkeeper

4

A. Answer these questions.

1. Why did Mrs. Jones go to town?
2. Which picture did she like most?
3. What did she say to the shopkeeper?
4. What did he say to Mrs. Jones?
5. What did she answer?

B. Which words in the story on page 4 mean the opposite of:

1. cheap
2. front
3. less
4. little
5. lot of
6. old

C. Put the number of the correct sentence under the correct picture.

1. He looked behind the picture and then said, 'Thirteen pounds.'
2. Mrs. Jones did not have a picture in her living-room.
3. She found a picture of a young girl.
4. She looked for a picture shop.
5. She said to the shopkeeper, 'How much is this?'
6. She went into the shop.
7. She went to town by bus.
8. Then she found one.

2

Mary worked in an office in London, and she usually went out and had lunch in a restaurant. She liked foreign food and often looked in the newspaper for the names of new restaurants, because she enjoyed going to them and eating new things. Sometimes she said, 'I don't like this restaurant. I'm not going to come here again'; but often she said, 'I like this one. I'm going to have my lunch here often.'

One day she saw the name of a new Greek restaurant in her newspaper, and she went there for lunch. It was very small, but it was clean and nice, and the food was good.

But then Mary found something hard in her mouth. She took it out. It was a button.

'Look here, waiter!' she said. 'I've found this button in my food.'

'Thank you, thank you!' the waiter answered happily. 'I looked everywhere for it.'

A. Answer these questions.

1. What food did Mary like?
2. Where did she go one day?
3. What did she find in her mouth?
4. What did she say then?
5. What did the waiter answer?

Words not in the 750: restaurant, thank you, waiter

B. Which of the answers to these questions are correct? Write the correct answers down.

1. Did Mary always go to the same restaurant?
   a. No, she didn't.
   b. Yes, she did.

2. Did she go back to a restaurant after the first time?
   a. No, never.
   b. Yes, always.
   c. Yes, often.

3. Where did she find the names of new restaurants?
   a. In a big city.
   b. In a newspaper.

4. What did she find in her mouth one day?
   a. A waiter's button.
   b. Some hard food.

5. Was the waiter happy, or angry?
   a. He was angry.
   b. He was happy.

C. Write this story. Put one word in each empty space. All the correct words are in the story on page 6.

This is Mary's brother. His ... is George. He lives in the ... of Chicago and works in a small ·Greek ... there. He is a .... A lot of people come and have ... there, because the ... is good. Look at that man. He is ... some meat and reading his .... He comes to this restaurant, because he works in an ... quite near here.

3

Peter was ten, and his sister Jane was eight. They lived in the country ten kilometres from Cardiff.

One day they saw a picture of a circus in the newspaper, and Jane said to her mother, 'There's going to be a circus in Cardiff next week. Please take us there.'

The children's mother bought tickets, and on Saturday evening Peter and Jane and their parents went to the circus.

The tent was full of people, and after a quarter of an hour, the circus began.

A beautiful young girl came in. She put a cake in her mouth, and then a big lion came and took the cake out of her mouth.

A man in a red coat shouted to the people, 'Who's going to do the same for £100?'

Nobody answered. But then a funny man stood up and said, 'All right... but first take the lion away!'

A. Answer these questions.

1. Where did the children and their parents go on Saturday evening?
2. What did the beautiful girl do?
3. What did the lion do?

Words not in the 750: circus, please

4. What did the man in a red coat say then?

5. And what did the funny man say?

B. Which of the words in the story on page 8 mean:

1. before that
2. men, women and children
3. said very loudly
4. the one after this one
5. very pretty

C. Find the right sentence for each picture. Write it down.

a. The girl is saying, 'Please bring me the cake now.'
b. The girl is saying, 'Please take me the cake now.'

a. The man is getting the girl the cake now.
b. The man is giving the girl the cake now.

a. A man is going to get the lion now.
b. A man is going to give the lion now.

a. The lion is bringing the cake.
b. The lion is taking the cake.

a. The man in the red coat is not going to get the funny man this money.
b. The man in the red coat is not going to give the funny man this money.

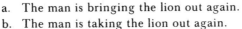
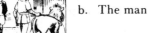
a. The man is bringing the lion out again.
b. The man is taking the lion out again.

9

4

Ann Grimes had a small car, and she drove a lot in town, because she went to work by car every morning and came home by car too, *and* she did her shopping with her car on Saturdays.

But she very seldom went out into the country in it, because she did not have much time.

Then one Sunday morning last August she said to herself, 'It's a beautiful day, and it's hot in town. I'm going to drive out into the country and have a picnic in a quiet field there.'

She drove twenty kilometres, and then she came to a small country road. She looked at it and said to herself, 'This road's very steep, isn't it?' She stopped in front of a house and asked a man, 'Is this road dangerous?'

'No,' the man answered, 'it isn't dangerous up here. They always crash down at the bottom.'

Words not in the 750:   circus, please

A. Answer these questions.

1. What did Ann say to herself one Sunday morning?
2. What did she come to after twenty kilometres?
3. What did she say to herself there?
4. What did she ask a man?
5. What did he answer?

B. Put *at*, *in*, or *on* in each empty space in these sentences:

1. Ann lived . . . a town.
2. She did her shopping . . . Saturdays.
3. She did it . . . the morning.
4. She went out into the country . . . Sunday morning.
5. She left her house . . . nine o'clock.
6. She said, 'I'm going to have a picnic . . . a field.'
7. She stopped her car . . . the gate of a small house.
8. The road was dangerous . . . the bottom.

C. Write this story.   Choose the correct words.

Ann never drives $\begin{Bmatrix} \text{dangerous} \\ \text{dangerously} \end{Bmatrix}$ She came to a $\begin{Bmatrix} \text{danger-} \\ \text{danger-} \end{Bmatrix}$ $\begin{Bmatrix} \text{ous} \\ \text{ously} \end{Bmatrix}$ road yesterday, and drove down it very $\begin{Bmatrix} \text{slow} \\ \text{slowly} \end{Bmatrix}$ Then she found a $\begin{Bmatrix} \text{quiet} \\ \text{quietly} \end{Bmatrix}$ field, and crossed it $\begin{Bmatrix} \text{quiet} \\ \text{quietly} \end{Bmatrix}$ There was a $\begin{Bmatrix} \text{beautiful} \\ \text{beautifully} \end{Bmatrix}$ river on the other side. Ann can draw $\begin{Bmatrix} \text{beautiful} \\ \text{beautifully} \end{Bmatrix}$, and she sat down at the side of the river

and began to draw a picture.

5

Paul Robinson liked fishing very much. In the summer he went out fishing every evening, and in the winter he fished on Saturdays and Sundays. His wife Joan did not see him very much.

Then one day last summer Paul said to her, 'I'm going to have two weeks' holiday this year, and we're going to go to Scotland and fish there.'

'And what am I going to do?' said Joan.

'You're going to fish with me,' Paul answered.

They went to Scotland and fished there for two weeks. Then they came home, and Joan talked to her neighbour, Mrs. Andrews, about her fishing trip with her husband.

'I did everything wrong on the trip,' she said to her. 'I talked loudly in the boat and the fish were afraid. I put the wrong things on my hook, I pulled my line in very quickly ... and I caught a lot more fish than Paul did.'

Word not in the 750: noise

12

A. Answer these questions.

1. What was Paul's hobby?
2. Where did he and his wife go last August?
3. What did they do for two weeks?
4. Who did Joan talk to after that?
5. What did Joan do wrong?

B. Which of these sentences are true? Write the correct ones down.

1. Paul loved fishing.
2. Paul hated fishing.
3. He fished very day.
4. He fished every day in the summer.
5. He was out of his house a lot.
6. He was with his wife most of the time.
7. He had two weeks' holiday alone.
8. He had two weeks' holiday with his wife.
9. She caught very few fish, because she did everything wrong.
10. She caught a lot of fish and that was the wrong thing to do.

C. Write this story, but do not put pictures. Put words.

Mr. and Mrs. Andrews went fishing. Mrs. Andrews wore

 . She took a food, and her husband

took a for the fish. Their was on the

 , but they pushed it into the , and Mr.

Andrews to an  Then he put a big

 on his  and began fishing.

13

6

Mrs. Davis lived near the sea, in Yarmouth, and went to the same fish shop there for twenty-five years. She always bought beautiful, fresh fish from that shop, but then she and her husband went to London and lived there. She wrote to her friends, 'I'm not going to find nice, fresh fish in the London shops. They lie there for days and weeks.'

There was a fish shop near her house, and she went and bought her fish there for two or three weeks, but she did not like them very much. Then last Wednesday, she went into the shop and looked at all the fish there.

'These ones aren't fresh,' she said to the shopkeeper. 'Look at them!'

The shopkeeper came and looked. Then he said angrily, 'That's your fault, not mine. These same fish were here in this shop last Friday, but you didn't buy them then, did you?'

A. Answer these questions.

1. What did Mrs. Davis write to her friends?

Words not in the 750: fault, fresh, shopkeeper

14

2. Where did she buy her fish for two or three weeks?
3. What did she do last Wednesday?
4. What did she say to the shopkeeper?
5. What did he answer?

B. Do this puzzle.

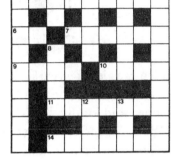

Across:
1. Mrs. Davis went into the fish shop last . . . .
6. Mrs. Davis lived ... London.
7. Most trees have these.
9. We have this on our heads.
10. The shopkeeper isn't very nice,......?
11. Mr. Davis was Mrs. Davis's . . . .
14. It's Monday today, so tomorrow is . . . .

Down:
1. Which fish do you want? Take ... one you like.
2. 'What ... you want?' the shopkeeper asked.
3. 'Do you ... have fresh fish in this shop?' Mrs. Davis said.
4. Mrs. ... wanted to buy fresh fish.
5. Today is Monday, so ... was Sunday.
8. There was always a lot of fresh ... in Yarmouth.
12. Mrs. Davis did not ... any fresh fish in the shop on Wednesday.
13. Mr. ... Mrs. Davis live in London now.

C. Draw lines from the words on the left to the right words on the right. Then write the five sentences.

1. Mr. Davis   a. bought fish from a shop in Yarmouth.
2. Mrs. Davis   b. did not have fresh fish.
3. The fish in Yarmouth   c. said, 'That's your fault.'
4. The fish shop in London d. was Mrs. Davis's husband.
5. The shopkeeper in London e. were very fresh.

15

7

Helen was eight years old, and one day one of her teeth began hurting. She cried in her class at school, and her teacher said kindly, 'Why are you crying, Helen?'

'Because one of my teeth hurts,' answered Helen.

'Speak to your mother about it,' said the teacher, 'and then go and see the dentist.'

That afternoon Helen spoke to her mother about her tooth, and her mother took her to the dentist a few days later. The dentist looked at the tooth and then he said to Helen, 'It's very bad. I'm going to take it out, and then you're going to get a nice, new tooth next year.' He pulled the tooth out.

The next day Helen's teacher asked her about the tooth. She said to her, 'Does it still hurt, Helen?'

'I don't know,' Helen answered.

'Why don't you know?' the teacher said.

'Because the dentist's got it,' Helen answered.

A. Answer these questions.

   1. What did the dentist do to Helen?
   2. What did her teacher ask the next day?
   3. What did Helen answer?
   4. What did the teacher ask then?
   5. And what did Helen answer?

Words not in the 750: know, still (adv.)

B. Which words in the story on page 16 mean the opposite of:

1. bring
2. earlier
3. good
4. laughed
5. morning
6. nastily
7. old
8. stopped

C. Put the number of the correct sentence under the correct picture.

1. Helen began to cry in her class.
2. Helen showed her her bad tooth.
3. Helen's mother took her to the dentist.
4. Her teacher said, 'Why are you crying, Helen?'
5. He said to Helen, 'Look at it. It's quite bad.'
6. The dentist looked in her mouth.
7. Then Helen went home with her mother.
8. Then he pulled the bad tooth out.

8

Mrs. Stephens lived in a small village, and she had five children. She always had a lot of work. The children went to different schools, and Mrs. Stephens took them there in the morning in her car. Then she bought food at the village shop, and then she went home and cleaned the house, washed the clothes and made cakes or other things.

In the afternoon she drove back to the children's schools and brought them home, and then she cooked their evening meal. Every evening she was very tired.

One morning she was in the village shop, and she saw a small notice there. It said, 'I do cleaning for £1.50 an hour. Telephone Miss Joan Brown, 7508.'

Mrs. Stephens looked around the shop. 'Nobody's looking,' she said. 'That's good.'

Then she took her pen out of her bag and wrote under the notice, 'I do cleaning for nothing. Don't telephone me!'

A. Answer these questions.

   1. Why did Mrs. Stephens always have a lot of work?
   2. What did she see in the village shop one morning?

Words not in the 750:   notice (n.), thing

3. What did the notice say?
4. What did Mrs. Stephens say?
5. And what did she write?

B. Which of the answers to these questions are right? Write the correct answers down.

1. Did Mrs. Stephens work hard?
   a. No, she didn't.
   b. Yes, she did.

2. Who took the children to school?
   a. Mr. Stephens.
   b. Mrs. Stephens.

3. Who cleaned Mrs. Stephens's house?
   a. Miss Joan Brown.
   b. Mrs. Stephens.

4. What did Miss Brown want?
   a. Work.
   b. A telephone.

5. How much money did Mrs. Stephens get for cleaning?
   a. Nothing.
   b. £1.50 an hour.

C. Write this story, but do not put pictures. Put words.

One day Mrs. Stephens went to the in the town.

She bought a small and some Then

she bought a for her tea, but the was

 After that, Mrs. Stephens bought a nice

for one of her daughters, and a for the other, and

a and some for the boys.

19

9

In hot, sunny countries, a lot of people like eating their meals in the fresh air. During the day, they eat under trees or big umbrellas, because the sun is usually very strong, but in the evening they eat under the moon and the stars.

People do this a lot in Italy. The restaurants put tables in a garden or in the street, and most people eat there and not in the restaurants.

Renato was an Italian. He came to London and bought a restaurant there. Then he said, 'I'm going to put some of my tables in the street here too.' But it rains a lot in England.

Mr. Jenkins went to Renato's restaurant one day, and in the evening he said to his wife, 'I had lunch at that new Italian restaurant today, and it rained all the time. Drinking my soup took twenty-five minutes.'

A. Answer these questions.

1. Where do people like eating in the fresh air?
2. What did Renato say?

Words not in the 750:   fresh, restaurant, soup

3. What did Mr. Jenkins do one day?
4. What was the weather like?
5. Why did drinking his soup take a long time?

B. Which words in the story on page 20 mean:

1. most of the time
2. clean
3. men, women and children
4. midday meal
5. more than half of the

C. Find the right sentence for each picture.   Write it down.

a. These boys ate their fish.
b. These boys hate their fish.

a. These boys ate their fish.
b. These boys hate their fish.

a. Two ears
b. Two years

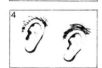

a. Two ears.
b. Two years.

a. That bus is very fast, but this one takes hours.
b. That bus is very fast, but this one takes ours.

a. That bus takes the other team, and this one takes hours.
b. That bus takes the other team, and this one takes ours.

21

10

Mac had a very old car. It was rusty and dirty, but its engine worked most of the time. One day he took his old car out of the garage and said to his wife, 'I'm going to drive to Bournemouth and do some shopping.'

He came to a quiet road after a few kilometres, but then his car stopped. Mac got out, opened the bonnet of the car and looked at the engine, but he did not find anything wrong with it.

His head was under the bonnet for quite a long time. Then a young man ran to the car and began pulling one of the red lights off the back of it.

Mac put his head up, looked at the young man and shouted, 'What are you doing there?'

The young man answered, 'You can steal the pieces at the front. I'm going to take the ones at the back.'

Words not in the 750: bonnet, rusty

A. Answer these questions.

1. What did Mac's car do on a quiet road?
2. What did Mac do then?
3. What did a young man do?
4. What did Mac shout?
5. And what did the young man answer?

B. Put *a few* or *a little* in each empty space in these sentences.

1. Mac drove ... kilometres. Then his car stopped.
2. He had ... money in his pocket for a bus.
3. He waited for ... minutes. Then a bus came.
4. It was ... slower than his car, but he got to a garage.
5. The man in the garage said to him, 'Wait ....'
6. Then he drove him back to his car with ... things in a bag.
7. He did ... work on the car, and then the engine began running.
8. Mac gave the man ... pounds and then drove on to Bournemouth.

C. Write these sentences. Choose the correct words.

1. This man is $\left\{ \begin{array}{c} \text{doing} \\ \text{making} \end{array} \right\}$ some work.

2. He·is $\left\{ \begin{array}{c} \text{doing} \\ \text{making} \end{array} \right\}$ a wall, but he has $\left\{ \begin{array}{c} \text{done} \\ \text{made} \end{array} \right\}$ a mistake. What is he going to $\left\{ \begin{array}{c} \text{do} \\ \text{make} \end{array} \right\}$ about it?

3. Now the other man is $\left\{ \begin{array}{c} \text{doing} \\ \text{making} \end{array} \right\}$ a fire, and his wife is going to $\left\{ \begin{array}{c} \text{do} \\ \text{make} \end{array} \right\}$ some tea on it.

4. What are they $\left\{ \begin{array}{c} \text{doing} \\ \text{making} \end{array} \right\}$ now? They are drinking their tea, and their small son is $\left\{ \begin{array}{c} \text{doing} \\ \text{making} \end{array} \right\}$ his homework.

23

11

George was an American. He went to Britain last summer, and he visited some of his British friends there. Two of them were Mr. and Mrs. Andrews. They lived near Edinburgh, and George stayed in their house for a week and enjoyed it very much.

On his last evening with the Andrews, George said to them, 'My aeroplane to New York leaves very early tomorrow morning. I'm going to get up at five o'clock and make my breakfast. Please don't come down.'

He said goodbye to his good friends that evening and came down to the kitchen in the morning and looked at the table. There was a photograph of Mrs. Andrews on it in front of her chair, and a photograph of Mr. Andrews in front of his chair.

George laughed happily and said, 'That's very good. I'm not going to eat my breakfast alone this morning!'

A. Answer these questions.

1. Why did Mr. and Mrs. Andrews not have breakfast with George on his last morning?
2. Why did he get up at five o'clock?
3. Who made the breakfast that day?

Word not in the 750: please

4. What did he find on the table in the kitchen?

5. What did he say then?

B. Which of these sentences are true?   Write the correct ones down.

1. George was a visitor to America.
2. George was a visitor to Britain.
3. Mr. and Mrs. Andrews were his host and hostess.
4. Mr. and Mrs. Andrews were his guests.
5. Mr. and Mrs. Andrews drove him to the airport.
6. Mr. and Mrs. Andrews stayed at home, and George went to the airport.
7. There were photographs of George on the table in the kitchen.
8. There were photographs of Mr. and Mrs. Andrews on the table in the kitchen.
9. George ate his breakfast with the photographs that morning.
10. George ate his breakfast with Mr. and Mrs. Andrews that morning.

C. Write this story, but do not put pictures.   Put words.

George went to London too. He visited the of

London, and London , and he went to the

 and to a One day he went to the

 , and another day he went round a car

Then he went to a big match. He had a good

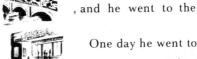 of London, but sometimes he asked a

the way somewhere. He liked the very much.

25

12

Mrs. Black had two coal fires in her house, and she always bought her coal from Mr. Matthews. He sold her good coal. There was never much dust in it.

But Mr. Matthews was old, and after a few years he stopped working in his coalyard, and his son Freddie began selling coal to Mrs. Black. He brought two sacks of coal to her house in his truck one day, and Mrs. Black said to him, 'Your father always sold me good coal. There was never much dust in the sacks.'

'I do that too,' young Mr. Matthews said.

A few months later he brought Mrs. Black another two sacks of coal and said to her, 'Did you find any dust in the last sacks of coal?'

'No, I didn't find *dust* in the sacks of *coal*,' answered Mrs. Black. 'I found some pieces of *coal* in the sacks of *dust*!'

A. Answer these questions.

1. What did Mrs. Black say to Freddie?
2. What did the young man answer?
3. What did he do a few months later?
4. What did he ask Mrs. Black?
5. What did she answer?

Words not in the 750: coalyard, sack

B. Do this puzzle.

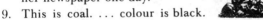

Across:

6. Mr. Matthews brought Mrs. Black two ... ...(three words)

7. Stop! The lights are ....

8. Mrs. Black ... about old Mr. Matthews in her newspaper one day.

9. This is coal. ... colour is black.

10. Young Mr. Matthews's first name.

12. Mother's mother.

Down:

1. 'Did Mrs. Black have any children?' 'Yes, she had one son and two ....'

2.

3. Mrs. Black has more fires in winter than in summer, because it is ... in winter.

4. Got a goal in football.

5. We buy newspapers every day, but we buy ... once a week or once a month.

11. 'Has Mrs. Black got ... coal in her sacks of dust?' 'Yes, she has some.'

13. Mrs. Black said, 'Please bring ... two more sacks of coal next month.'

14. 'It's late. Go ... bed.

C. Draw lines from the words on the left to the correct words on the right. Then write the four sentences.

1. Mrs. Black   a. always sold Mrs. Black good coal.
2. Old Mr. Matthews   b. bought coal from Mr. Matthews.
3. The sacks of coal   c. sold Mrs. Black a lot of coal dust.
4. Young Mr. Matthews   d. had coal and dust in them.

27

13

Mr. Gray went to work by train every day and he always walked from the station to his office. It was about one kilometre, and he never went by bus, because he enjoyed walking fast. It sometimes rained or snowed, but then Mr. Gray put his umbrella up, turned the collar of his coat up, and walked fast.

There was always a poor man at the side of a narrow street near Mr. Gray's office. He had one leg, and he sold matches in the street. A box of them cost 20p. Mr. Gray always smiled at the poor man and said, 'Good morning.' Then he gave him 20p and did not take any of his matches, because he did not smoke.

One day Mr. Gray gave the poor man his 20p and began walking on, but the man shouted after him, 'Sir, the matches cost 25p now!'

A. Answer these questions.

1. Who did Mr. Gray always see in the street?
2. What did Mr. Gray always say and do?
3. Did he take any matches?
4. Why?

Word not in the 750: sir

5. What did the poor man shout after him one day?

B. Which words in the story on page 28 mean the opposite of:

1. bought
2. give
3. never
4. night
5. rich
6. said very quietly
7. slowly
8. wide

C. Put the number of the correct sentence under the correct picture.

1. But the poor man shouted, 'They cost 25p now!'
2. He gave 20p to the poor man.
3. He got out in London.
4. He sold matches there every day.
5. It was snowing, but he walked to his office.
6. Mr. Gray got on his train.
7. Then he walked on.
8. There was a poor man in the street.

14

Neil was five years old, and he had no brothers or sisters. He lived with his parents in the country, and there were no neighbours near his house.

One Saturday Neil's Uncle Fred came and visited them. He had lunch with Neil and his parents, and then Neil's mother went into the kitchen and washed the dishes, and his father went out and washed the car.

'Stay here and talk to Uncle Fred,' Neil's father said to him.

'And show him your toys,' his mother said.

Neil showed his uncle his toys and they talked for half an hour in the living-room. Then Neil said to his uncle, 'I'm going to go out and play with God in the garden now.'

His uncle was surprised. 'How do you play with God, Neil?' he asked him.

'It's easy,' Neil answered. 'I throw the ball up, and then God throws it back down to me.'

Words not in the 750: God, surprised

A. Answer these questions.

1. Who had lunch with Neil and his parents one day?
2. What did Neil and his uncle do in the living-room?
3. What did Neil say then?
4. What did Uncle Fred ask Neil?
5. And what did Neil answer?

B. Which of the answers to these questions are correct? Write the correct answers down.

1. How many children did Neil's parents have?
   a. More than one.
   b. One.

2. How many people lived near Neil's house?
   a. A few.
   b. A lot.
   c. None.

3. What did Neil's father do after lunch?
   a. He cleaned his car.
   b. He sat in the living-room and talked to Uncle Fred.

4. What did Neil do after lunch?
   a. He stayed in the living-room and talked to Uncle Fred.
   b. He went into the kitchen and washed the dishes with his mother.

5. How did Neil play with God?
   a. He hit his ball and then ran and got it.
   b. He threw his ball up and then caught it.

C. Write this story. Put one word in each empty space. All the correct words are in the story on page 30.

Joan Brown is a small girl. Her ... are Mr. George Brown and his wife Dorothy. They live in a nice ... in the ..., and their ... on both sides have children. Joan is going to ... with them this afternoon, but first she is washing the ... with her mother in their small .... Joan has a lot of ..., but she likes playing ball with her friends in her ... the best of all. They ... it to each other and catch it.

31

15

George and Jack were friends and neighbours. They were both policemen, and they sometimes went out together in a police car and drove around in town for a few hours.

One evening they got into the car at the police station and drove around from eight o'clock to midnight. First the town was quite quiet, but then, at half past eleven, there were a few drunk people in the streets.

George stopped the car, and Jack went to them and said, 'Go home.'

Then there was another drunk man. George said to Jack, 'Look, Jack. That man's going round and round a tree, and he's knocking at it all the time.'

He stopped the car, and Jack got out and went to the man. 'Go home,' he said to him.

The drunk man stopped, looked at Jack for a few seconds and then answered, 'Don't be stupid! There's a wall right round me.'

A. Answer these questions.

    1. What did George and Jack do one evening?
    2. Who did they see in the streets at half past eleven?

Word not in the 750: drunk

3. What did George say to Jack after that?
4. What did Jack say to the drunk man?
5. And what did the drunk man answer?

B. Which of the words in the story on page 32 mean:

1. about
2. in the beginning
3. to your house
4. twelve o'clock at night
5. with each other

C. Find the right sentence for each picture. Write it down.

a. This man is knocking at a tree.
b. This man is knocking a nail into a tree.
c. This man is knocking a tree down.

a. This man is knocking at a tree.
b. This man is knocking a nail into a tree.
c. This man is knocking a tree down.

a. This man is knocking at a tree.
b. This man is knocking a nail into a tree.
c. This man is knocking a tree down.

a. This man has drunk some water.
b. This man is drinking.
c. This man is drunk.

a. This man has drunk some water.
b. This man is drinking.
c. This man is drunk.

a. This man has drunk some water.
b. This man is drinking.
c. This man is drunk.

33

16

Mr. and Mrs. Richards were young, and they loved dancing and loud music, but they did not have very much money. They lived in a small flat and had a small stereo. They listened to it every evening and all the time on Saturdays and Sundays.

Mr. and Mrs. Richards both worked hard in a shop, and after a year they had quite a lot of money. Then they went out and bought a big, new stereo. It played music much more loudly than the old one. Mr. and Mrs. Richards sometimes played music very loudly at night and danced in their living-room for hours.

Then one day Mrs. Richards met one of their neighbours on the stairs and said to her, 'We've got a beautiful new stereo now. Come to our flat and listen to it this evening.'

'No,' the neighbour answered, 'come to *our* flat and listen to it there!'

Words not in the 750: flat (n.), stereo

A. Answer these questions.

1. How did Mr. and Mrs. Richards get quite a lot of money?
2. What did they buy?
3. Who did Mrs. Richards meet on the stairs?
4. What did she say to her?
5. And what did the neighbour answer?

B. Put one of these words in each empty space in these sentences:

our, ours, us, we, you, your, yours

1. Mrs. Richards said, '. . . have a new stereo.'
2. Then she said, 'Come and listen to it in . . . flat.'
3. 'No, come and listen to it in . . . !' her neighbour answered.
4. 'Come and visit . . . this evening.'
5. 'Have . . . got a stereo too?' Mrs. Richards asked.
6. 'No, we listen to . . . , but not in . . . flat.'

C. Write this story, but do not put pictures. Put words.

George loves . It is his hobby. He listens to it

on his , but he wants a big, new too.

He loves listening to good

This is George's , Eliza. She is an

She paints beautiful . She also makes

of animals and sells them. George has brought his

and is taking a of some of them now.

35

17

George never liked work very much. At school he was always at the bottom of his class. Then he went and worked in an office, but he did not do much work there.

There were big windows in the office, and there was a street below them. There were always a lot of people and cars and buses in the street, and George liked sitting at his desk and looking at them.

George had a friend. His name was Peter, and he worked in the same office, but he was very different from George. He worked very hard.

Last Tuesday George stood at one of the windows of the office for a long time. Then he said to his friend Peter, 'There's a very lazy man in the street. He began digging a hole this morning, but he hasn't done any work for half an hour.'

A. Answer these questions.

1. Who was Peter?
2. How was he different from George?
3. What did George do for half an hour last Tuesday?
4. What did he say to Peter then?
5. Who were the lazy people?

B. Which of these sentences are true? Write the correct ones down.

1. George was a lazy man.
2. George always worked very hard.
3. George cleaned the windows in an office.
4. George worked at a desk in an office.
5. George looked at the people and cars in the street from his office window.
6. George went to the other side of the street and looked at the people and cars from there.
7. Peter worked in the street in front of the office.
8. Peter and George worked in the same office.
9. The man in the street was as lazy as Peter.
10. The man in the street was as lazy as George.

C. Write this story. Put one of these words in each empty space:

all, both, neither, none

George has two brothers. ... of his brothers likes hard work: ... of them are very lazy. But Peter has three sisters too, and ... of them work hard and enjoy it. ... of them is lazy. They had a lot of work yesterday. They worked very hard and finished ... of it before 6 p.m. They left ... of it for the next day.

18

Tim Jackson was a rich young man. He liked girls very much and often went out to dinner with them.

He usually went to the same restaurant, but the waiters there did not like him very much, because he did not give them good tips, and because he always asked them difficult questions and then gave them the answers. Then the girls laughed and said, 'You are clever, Tim!' and Tim was happy.

One day he took a beautiful girl to the restaurant. Her name was Susan. Tim said to her, 'What are you going to eat, Susan?'

She looked at everything and then said, 'Those fish look good, don't they?'

Tim looked at them and said, 'Yes, they do. I know a lot about fish.' Then he turned to the waiter and said, 'Waiter, these fish are French, aren't they?'

'I don't know,' answered the waiter. 'They haven't spoken to me.'

A. Answer these questions.

1. What did Tim ask Susan in the restaurant?·
2. What did Susan say to Tim?
3. And what did he answer?
4. What did he say to the waiter?
5. And what did the waiter answer?

Words not in the 750: know, tip (n.), waiter

B. Do this puzzle.

Across:

1. Tim often had his lunch in . . . .
7. This waiter is . . . his tips.
8. 'Are you our waiter?' 'Yes, I . . . .'
9. 1.
10. Tim gets up at 7.00, and Susan at 7.30. Tim gets up . . . than Susan.
11. This man is very . . . .
12. The young man's name was . . . Jackson.
13. People usually eat their meals in their . . . .

Down:

1. Tim has more money than his friends. He is . . . than they are.
2. Tim left school a few years ago, and then he was a . . . at a university.
3. Between midday and the evening.
4. Tim is . . . now.
5. . . . fish speak French.
6. Not often.
8. There are 60 minutes in . . . hour.
9. 'Do you want meat, . . . fish?'
12. Susan ate some fish, and Tim ate some fish . . . .

C. Draw lines from the words on the left to the correct words on the right. Then write the five sentences.

1. Susan   a. liked Tim because he did not give good tips.
2. None of the waiters   b. never said anything.
3. One of the waiters   c. often went out to dinner with girls.
4. The fish   d. said, 'I don't know.'
5. Tim   e. was a beautiful girl.

39

19

It was a very hot day in the middle of summer, and there were no trees along the street. Mr. Brown closed his shop at half past five, went out into the street and began walking to his bus. He was very fat. The sun shone straight down the street, and in a few minutes Mr. Brown was very hot.

A small boy came out of another shop in the street and followed Mr. Brown. He stayed very near him all the time, and he kicked the heels of Mr. Brown's shoes several times. Mr. Brown looked at him angrily each time.

After the third time, Mr. Brown stopped, turned round and said to the small boy, 'What are you doing? Stop following me like that! You're going to hurt my heels.'

'Please don't stop me!' the small boy said. 'It's very hot today, and there isn't any shade anywhere else in the street!'

A. Answer these questions.

    1. Why was Mr. Brown very hot in the street?
    2. Who came out of another shop?

Words not in the 750: heel, please, shade (n.)

3. What did the boy do?
4. What did Mr. Brown say after the third time?
5. What did the boy answer?

B. Which words in the story on page 40 mean the opposite of:

1. cold
2. far from
3. big
4. thin
5. sun
6. winter

C. Put the number of the correct sentence under the correct picture.

1. A small boy came out of another shop.
2. He began walking to his bus.
3. He followed Mr. Brown.
4. He kicked Mr. Brown's heels.
5. He went out into the street.
6. Mr. Brown closed his shop.
7. Mr. Brown stopped and spoke to him angrily.
8. There were no trees in the street.

20

Harry has always loved aeroplanes. When he was younger, he said, 'I'm going to go into the Air Force,' but his eyes were not very good, and he did not get in.

Then he said, 'I'm going to buy a small aeroplane, and I'm going to have flying lessons,' but small aeroplanes and flying lessons are very expensive, and Harry did not have much money.

But last year Harry found a new skydiver's club near his home. The lessons did not cost very much, and Harry began going to the club every Saturday and Sunday and having lessons. Now he is a good skydiver.

Last week an old lady said to him, 'You're a very brave young man. How do you jump out of an aeroplane like that?'

' I'm not brave,' Harry said and he smiled. 'I'm in the aeroplane, and I say to myself, "It's going to crash in a few seconds!" Then I'm very afraid, and I jump out quickly.'

Words not in the 750: crash (v.), skydiver

A. Answer these questions.

1. What did Harry do at the club?
2. What is he now?
3. What did a woman ask him last week?
4. What does Harry always say to himself in an aeroplane?
5. What does he do then? Why?

B. Which of the answers to these questions are correct? Write the correct answers.

1. Did Harry go into the Air Force?
   a. No, because he was afraid.
   b. No, because his eyes are not very good.
   c. Yes.

2. Did he buy a small aeroplane?
   a. No, because he is not a rich man.
   b. No, because his eyes are not very good.
   c. Yes.

3. Did he have lessons at the skydivers' club?
   a. No, because they were on Saturdays and Sundays.
   b. No, because they were very expensive.
   c. Yes.

4. Why does he jump out of the aeroplane quickly?
   a. Because he is afraid.
   b. Because he is brave.

C. Write this story. Put one word in each empty space. All the correct words are in the story on page 42.

When David was a boy, his hobby was making model .... He was not rich, but making them was not very .... He enjoyed ... his models in a field near his house. They went up into the ... like big aeroplanes, and sometimes they fell and hit the ground with a big .... When he was older, he found a flying ... near his home, and he had some ... there. Sometimes the wind threw the small aeroplane around, but he was never ..., because he was a ... young man. Once he nearly crashed, and his teacher said, '...!', but he did not, and the aeroplane came down quite well.

43

21

Jill was four years old. She was a clever child, but she was not very pretty. She went to school every day, and she loved her lessons. She was always at the top of her class, and she learnt to read and write very quickly.

One day her mother said to her, 'Aunt Kathy and Aunt Judy are going to visit us tomorrow. They live in Canada, and you haven't met them, because they very seldom come to England. They're going to have lunch with us.'

The aunts arrived at twelve o'clock the next day, and Jill's mother gave them some coffee. Then she said, 'I'm going to make lunch now,' and went into the kitchen. Jill stayed in the living-room with her aunts.

Aunt Kathy looked at Jill and then said to Aunt Judy quietly, 'She isn't very p-r-e-t-t-y, is she?'

'No,' said Jill quickly, 'but I'm very c-l-e-v-e-r.'

A. Answer these questions.

1. What did Jill's mother say to her one day?
2. When did the aunts arrive?
3. What did Jill's mother give them?
4. What did Aunt Judy say about Jill?
5. And what did Jill answer?

B. Which of the words in the story on page 44 mean:

1. beautiful
2. best pupil
3. come and see
4. liked very much
5. mother's or father's sister

C. Find the right sentence for each picture. Write it down.

a. Jill is sitting on a table.
b. Jill is sitting on a chair.

a. Jill is sitting at a desk.
b. Jill is sitting at a table.

a. Jill is sitting at a desk.
b. Jill is sitting at a table.

a. Jill's books are on a cupboard.
b. Jill's books are in a cupboard.

a. Jill's books are on a cupboard.
b. Jill's books are in a cupboard.

22

Mrs. Grace was forty. One day she said to her husband, 'I weighed myself this morning. I weigh seventy kilos.'

'Is that bad?' answered Mr. Grace.

'Yes, it is.' Mrs. Grace said. 'It's very bad. Each week I'm heavier now. I'm going to eat less, and I'm going to have a walk every day.'

The next morning she put her coat on and began walking, but during her walk it rained, and the rain went through her coat.

That evening she said to her husband, 'I want a good coat for my walks. I'm going to go to the shops tomorrow, and I'm going to buy one.'

The next morning she went into a shop and looked at some coats with the salesgirl. She liked a seal coat very much.

'This seal coat's nice,' she said to the salesgirl, 'but does the rain come through it?'

The salesgirl smiled and answered, 'Have you ever seen a seal with an umbrella?'

Words not in the 750: salesgirl, seal (n.)

A. Answer these questions.

1. What did the rain do during Mrs. Grace's first walk?
2. What did she say to her husband that evening?
3. What did she do the next morning?
4. What did she say to the salesgirl?
5. What did the salesgirl answer?

B. Put one of these in each empty space in the sentences:

drives, has, is driving, is having, is putting, puts

Mrs. Grace ... her husband to the station now. She ... him there every day.

Mrs. Grace ... her coat on now. She always ... it on before a walk.

Mrs. Grace ... for a walk now. She ... for a walk every morning.

C. Write this story. Put one of these words in each empty space:

angry, clothes, club, dance, fat, put, said, sizes, thin, went

Why do some girls not eat much? Because they like being ... and not .... Last autumn, Mrs. Grace's daughter ate a lot, and then she took some of her ... out of her cupboard and said, 'I'm going to ... this dress on now,' but it did not go over her head. Then she was ... and ... , 'I'm going to go to a ... at the young people's ... tonight, and I haven't got a dress!' Then she ... to a shop. They had dresses of lots of different.... She bought one and then she said, 'I'm not going to eat any-thing for a week — after the dance!'

23

Ted worked in a factory, but he was not very good, and he lost his job one day. His wife looked in the newspaper and said, 'One of the banks wants a guard.'

'I'm going to go there tomorrow,' Ted said, 'and I'm going to ask for that job. It's quite an easy one, and I'm quite strong.'

The next morning he went to the bank at half past nine and said, 'I want that job here. The guard's job.'

A man gave him a piece of paper. There were a lot of questions on it. 'Write your answers under the questions,' the man said to Ted.

One of the questions was, 'Have you ever been in prison?'

Ted smiled happily and wrote 'No' under this question.

Then he looked at the next question. It was 'Why?'

He thought for a long time and then he wrote, 'Because the police have never caught me.'

Words not in the 750:   guard (n.), job, police, prison

A. Answer these questions.

1. What did the man at the bank do, and what did he say to Ted?
2. What was one question on the piece of paper?
3. What did Ted answer?
4. What was the next question?
5. And what was Ted's answer?

B. Which of these sentences are true? Write the correct ones down.

1. Ted worked very well in the factory.
2. Ted did not work well in the factory.
3. He lost his job, and then he went to another factory and asked for work.
4. He lost his job, and then he went to a bank and asked for work.
5. He wanted a guard's job.
6. He wanted a bank clerk's job.
7. Ted was never in prison.
8. Ted was in prison once.
9. The police caught him.
10. The police never caught him.

C. How is the first picture different from the second one? Use these words and finish the sentences:

raining, shining, waiting, wearing

In A, ...   In B, ...

In A, ...   In B, ...

In A, ...   In B, ...

49

24

Ken was fifty, and his wife Liz was forty-eight. They had a very old car.

'I'm going to sell this car,' Ken said to Liz last month, but nobody wanted it, because it was old and did not run well.

Last Friday, Ken said to Liz, 'I've got some work in Boxbury. Come with me and do your shopping there.'

Liz was very happy, because her husband very seldom took her out, and she usually shopped in their small village.

Ken drove their old car to the River Dee. There was a ferry there, and cars and trucks crossed on it to the other side. It was the shortest way to Boxbury.

The ferryman came to Ken and said, 'A pound for the car and twenty-five pence for the passenger.'

Ken answered, 'Take the car for a pound, but I'm not going to sell my wife for less than fifty pence.'

Words not in the 750: ferry, ferryman

50

A. Answer these questions.

1. What did Ken say to his wife last Friday?
2. Why was she happy then?
3. Where did Ken drive first?
4. What did the ferryman say to him?
5. And what did Ken answer?

B. Do this puzzle.

Across:

5. Each ... on the ferry paid 25p.
6. 'We don't ... your car, because it's old,' everyone said.
7. Liz does not cook with electricity or gas. She cooks with ....
8. The ferry crossed this river.
9. 'I'm going to ... shopping,' Liz said.
11. 'Ladies and ..., the ferry's going to leave in five minutes.'

Down:

1. Fathers, mothers, sons and daughters.
2. 'How much does this cost?' Liz ....
3. 'Two pounds,' the man in the fish shop ....
4. The old car ... to Ken.
10. Ken and Liz crossed the river ... a ferry.
12. Our house is ten kilometres ... the south of Boxbury.

C. Draw lines from the words on the left to the correct words on the right. Then write the five sentences.

1. Boxbury	a. asked Ken for £1.25.
2. Ken	b. cost one pound for a car.
3. Liz	c. wanted to do her shopping in Boxbury.
4. The ferry	d. had some work in Boxbury.
5. The ferryman	e. was on the other side of the river.

51

25

Mr. Brown had a beautiful shop. He sold sweets and a lot of children came and bought them after school, but some of them looked into the window of the shop first, and put their fingers on the glass, and Mr. Brown did not like dirty windows.

Then last week he made a big notice. On it he wrote, 'Children! Do not put your fingers on this glass! It is dangerous!' And then he put it up in the window of his shop.

The shop on Mr. Brown's left was a shoe shop, and his friend, Tom Jones, worked there. Tom saw the notice and was surprised. He went into Mr. Brown's shop and said to him, 'Why is the glass in your shop window dangerous, Alf? What does it do to the children?'

Mr. Brown smiled. 'The glass doesn't do anything to the children, Tom,' was his answer, 'but *I* give them a hard smack.'

A. Answer these questions.

1. What did Mr. Brown sell in his shop?
2. What did some of the children do?
3. What did Mr. Brown write on his notice?
4. What did Tom ask Mr. Brown?

Words not in the 750: notice (n.), smack (n.)

5. And what did Mr. Brown answer?

B. Which of the words in the story on page 52 mean the opposite of:

1. before
2. clean
3. out of
4. question
5. right
6. soft
7. take
8. ugly

C. Put the number of the correct sentence under the correct picture.

1. He looked at the notice.
2. His friend Tom came out of the next shop.
3. Mr. Brown answered, 'It isn't.'
4. Mr. Brown cleaned his shop window.
5. Mr. Brown was angry and smacked them.
6. Some children put their fingers on it.
7. Then he put a notice in his window.
8. Then he said to Mr. Brown, 'Why is the glass dangerous?'

26

Dick Leonard was the captain of a small ship, the 'London Flower'. Sometimes it took engines from one port to another, sometimes it took furniture, and sometimes it took other things. But sometimes there was no work for it, and the ship was empty. Then Captain Leonard was not happy, because he loved being busy, and he loved going from one port to another all the time.

But the other men on the ship were lazy. They did not like work much. They liked sitting and doing nothing.

One day Captain Leonard did not see two of them for a long time. He looked for them. He opened a door and shouted down some stairs, 'Who's there?'

'William, Captain,' was the answer.

'What are you doing there, William?' the captain asked.

'Nothing, Captain,' William answered.

'Is Tom there?' the captain shouted then.

'Yes, he is,' was the answer.

'What's he doing?' the captain asked.

'He's helping me, Captain,' William answered.

A. Answer these questions.

    1. What were the first question and answer?
    2. What were the second question and answer?
    3. What were the third question and answer?

Words not in the 750: busy, help (v.)

4. What was Captain Leonard's last question?
5. And what was William's answer?

B. Which of the answers to these questions are correct? Write the correct answers.

1. Did Dick Leonard enjoy being a captain?

   a. No, he didn't.
   b. Yes, a little.
   c. Yes, very much.

2. Did the other men on the ship like hard work?

   a. No, they did not.
   b. Yes, they liked it a little.
   c. Yes, they liked it very much.

3. Was William busy?

   a. No, he was not.
   b. Yes, he was.

4. Where was Tom?

   a. He was with the captain.
   b. He was with William.

5. Was Tom busy?

   a. No, he was not.
   b. Yes, he was.

C. Write this story. Put one word in each empty space. All the correct words are in the story on page 54.

Dick Leonard's friend Joe is a ... too. His ... is the 'Brighton Flower'. It is not doing any voyages now, because its ... have broken. It is in a small ... in the south of England. Joe enjoys doing nothing, because he is a ... man. He does not like hard ... much. Some men are working on the ship's engines, and they are always very .... They are running up and down the ... now, but Joe is not ... them. He is looking at his glass. It is ..., and he is saying, 'I'm going to get another drink now.'

27

Mr. Hughes lived twenty kilometres from London, and his office was in the City. He went to work by train and bus at 8.00 in the morning and got home at 7.30 in the evening.

It rains rather a lot in England, and Mr. Hughes usually took an umbrella with him to London, but he often lost umbrellas. He lost them in buses, in trains and in shops. His wife often said to him, 'Umbrellas are expensive, David, and you buy one every week. Bring this one home this evening!'

One evening Mr. Hughes saw an umbrella in his train. 'Today I'm not going to lose my umbrella,' he said happily, and he took the umbrella, got out of the train at his station and brought the umbrella home.

His wife saw it and began laughing. 'But, David,' she said, 'you didn't take an umbrella with you this morning. That one isn't yours!'

A. Answer these questions.

1. What did Mr. Hughes often do with umbrellas?
2. What did his wife say?
3. What did he see in his train one evening?
4. What did he say and do?

5. What did his wife say then?

B. Which of the words in the story on page 56 mean:
1. between afternoon and night
2. costing a lot of money
3. each
4. many times
5. to his house

C. Find the right sentence for each picture and write it down.

    a. Mr. Hughes's umbrella is in his hand.
    b. Mr. Hughes's umbrella is on his arm.

    a. Mr. Hughes's umbrella is in his hand.
    b. Mr. Hughes's umbrella is on his arm.

    a. There is a fly on Mr. Hughes's foot.
    b. There is a fly on Mr. Hughes's leg.

    a. Now it is on his foot.
    b. Now it is on his leg.

    a. Mr. Hughes is looking at a clock.
    b. Mr. Hughes is looking at a watch.

    a. Mr. Hughes is looking at a clock.
    b. Mr. Hughes is looking at a watch.

28

Edward was at school. He was sixteen, and he lived with his mother and father near London. Then he left school and worked in a factory for a year, and then in August he said to his parents, 'I'm going to have a nice holiday in the country now, and I'm going to go there alone.'

He did not have much money, but he found the name of a small, cheap hotel, and he went there by train and bus. His room in the hotel was very small, but it was clean, and Edward was happy, because he was alone.

The first evening, he went down to the dining-room of the hotel at dinner time and sat down at a small table. The young waitress brought him a plate, and Edward looked at it. Then he said to the girl, 'Waitress, this plate's wet!'

'That's your soup,' the girl answered.

Words not in the 750: soup, waitress

A. Answer these questions.

1. Why did Edward go to a cheap hotel?
2. Where did he have dinner the first evening?
3. What did the young waitress bring him?
4. What did he say to her?
5. And what did she answer?

B. Put *a*, *an*, **or** *the* **in each empty space in these sentences.**

1. Edward looked for . . . cheap hotel and found one.
2. . . . name of . . . hotel was . . . Apollo.
3. . . . first evening, Edward went into . . . dining-room of . . . hotel.   There was . . . young waitress there.
4. . . . waitress brought Edward . . . plate.
5. . . . plate was wet.   That was Edward's soup.
6. Then Edward had . . . piece of meat.
7. And then he had . . . apple.
8. . . . apple was nice.
9. Next morning, Edward sat in . . . sun and read . . . book.
10. . . . book was about . . . City of New York.

C. Write this story, but do not put pictures.   Put words.

Edward's father spent a week in a big   It had

a   and he had a nice room with a , a

   and a   The    was nice but

small.   On the first evening, he had   for dinner,

and on the second evening,

59

29

Jack was five years old. His small friends had cats and dogs in their houses, but Jack's parents did not have any animals.

Then one day Jack said to his mother, 'I want a cat, Mummy.'

His mother did not say 'Yes' or 'No'. First, she wanted to talk to her husband.

That evening she said to her husband, 'Joe, all Jack's friends have got dogs or cats, and we have no animals. Now Jack wants one.'

'A cat's easier than a dog, Helen,' her husband answered.

'Our neighbours' cat's going to have kittens,' Helen said. 'They aren't going to want them all.'

'Good,' answered Joe. 'Ask them for one.'

A few days later, the neighbour's cat had four kittens, and after a few weeks, the neighbours gave one to Jack's mother.

But then Jack pulled the kitten's tail, and his mother said to him, 'Don't pull the kitten's tail, Jack!'

Jack answered, 'I'm not pulling it, Mummy. I'm holding it, and the kitten's pulling.'

Words not in the 750: kitten, Mummy

A. Answer these questions.

1. What did Jack say to his mother one day?
2. Where did Jack's kitten come from?
3. What did Jack do to the kitten?
4. What did his mother say to him then?
5. And what did he answer?

B. Which of these sentences are true? Write the correct ones down.

1. Jack's small friends did not have any cats or dogs in their houses.
2. Jack's small friends had some animals.
3. Jack wanted a cat.
4. Jack wanted a dog.
5. Jack's father said, 'Dogs are easier than cats.'
6. Jack's father said, 'Cats are easier than dogs.'
7. A neighbour's cat brought Jack one of her kittens.
8. Some neighbours gave Jack one kitten.
9. Some neighbours gave Jack four kittens.
10. The kitten pulled its tail.

C. Write these sentences. Put one of these words in each empty space:

How, What, Where, Which, Who, Whose, Why

a. '... kitten is this?' 'It is Jack's.'
b. '... colour is it?' 'It's black.'
c. '... did Jack want a kitten?' 'Because all his friends had animals.'

a. '... is Jack doing to the kitten? 'He's pulling its tail.'
b. '... is talking to him?' 'His mother is.'
c. '... is she saying?' 'Don't pull the kitten's tail!'

a. '... is the kitten now?' 'In the garden.'
b. '... did it get out of the house?' 'Through a window.'
c. '... way is it going now?' 'To the left.'

61

30

Joe Smith sold his house and bought a new one. He put all his furniture in a truck and drove to the new house. There he drove the truck into the garage and took the furniture out. Then the truck was empty, and Joe looked at it.

'The truck's higher now, because it's empty,' he said to himself. 'It isn't going to get out of the garage again.' He began driving it out very slowly, but it hit the top of the door.

Joe said, 'What am I going to do now?' But then he went to all his new neighbours and said, 'Please come and sit in my truck.'

They were surprised, but they went and sat in the truck. It was heavy now, and Joe drove it out of the garage easily.

The neighbours were happy, and Joe was happy too. 'Now all of us are friends!' he said.

Words outside the 750: please, surprised.

A. Answer these questions.

1. Why did the truck hit the top of the door?
2. What did Joe say to his neighbours then?
3. And what did they do?
4. Why did the truck not hit the top of the door now?
5. What did Joe say then?

B. Do this puzzle.

Across:

5. Joe took his ... to his new house in a truck.

6.

8. There is ... furniture in Joe's truck now.

9. This ship's officer is a ....

12. These are ....

Down:

1.

2. Joe's neighbours sat ... his truck.
3. Jimmy is the ..., dirtiest boy in school!
4. The lights are ... now. Go!

7. Joe Smith is the ... of Fred and Alice Smith.
10. ... round and look behind you.
11. Joe's ... house was not far from his old one.

C. Draw lines from the words on the left to the correct words on the right. Then write the five sentences.

1. Joe
2. Joe's furniture
3. Joe's neighbours
4. The top of the door
5. The truck

a. hit the top of the door.
b. stopped the truck getting out.
c. took his furniture to his new house.
d. was in the truck with Joe.
e. were very heavy.

APPENDIX

A 750-Word Vocabulary

Note: This vocabulary does not contain numerals, names of the days of the week, names of the months or proper nouns and adjectives. Not all cases of nouns and pronouns are given (e.g. *boy* stands for *boy—boy's—boys —boys'*; *I* stands for *I—me— my—mine*); nor are all parts of verbs given (e.g. *swim* stands for *swim—swims—swam—swum —swimming*).* Comparatives and superlatives of adjectives and adverbs are also not given.

The abbreviation a. means adjective and/or adverb; n. means noun; and v. means verb.

Words outside this list are printed at the bottom of the pages on which they are used— for example, *offer* on page 4.

a[n]	around	bear (*n.*)	bottom
about	arrive	beard	bowl (*n.*)
above	artist	beat (*v*)	box (*n.*)
absent (*a.*)	as	beautiful	boy
across	ask	because	brave
address (*n.*)	asleep	bed	bread
aeroplane	at	before	break
afraid	attack	begin[ning]	breakfast
after	aunt	behind	bridge
afternoon	autumn	bell	bright
again	awake	belong	bring
against	away	belt	broken
ago		bench	brother
air [force]		between	brown
[hostess]	baby	bicycle	brush
[port]	back (*a.*)	big	bucket
all	back (*n.*)	bird	bunch
almost	bad (worse, worst)	black	burst
alone	bag	blackboard	bus
along	ball	blanket	bush
always	balloon	blouse	but
a.m.	banana	blue	butter
among	bank	boat	button
and	bar	body (*and* -body,	buy
angry	barber	*e.g. in* anybody)	by
animal	basin	bomb	
answer	basket	book	
any	bath	boot	cage
apple	bathe	born	cake
arm	be	both	camera
army	beach	bottle	camp

64

can (v)
cap
captain
car
card
carpet
carriage
cart
cat
catch
ceiling
chair
chalk
cheap
cheese
chicken
child
chimney
cigarette
cinema
circle
city
class
clean
clerk
clever
climate
climb
clock
close (v)
clothes
cloud[y]
club
coat
coffee
cold
collar
colour
comb
come
cook
cool
corner
correct
cost
cotton
cough
count (v)
country
cow
cross (n.)

cross (v)
crowd
cry
cup
cupboard
curtain
cut
cycle (v)

damp
dance
dark
date
daughter
day
dead
deep
dentist
desk
different
difficult
dining[-room/-hall]
dinner
dirty
dish
do
doctor/Dr
dog
donkey
door
double
down
draw
dream
dress
drink
drive
drop (v)
dry
duck
during
dust[y]
duster

each
ear
early
east
easy

eat
egg
electric[ity]
elephant
else
empty
end
enemy
engine
enjoy
equal
evening
ever
every
examination
except
exercise
expensive
eye

face
factory
fall
family
far
fast
fat
father
few
field
fight
film
find
fine (a.)
finish
fire
first
fish[erman]
flag
floor
flower
fly (n.)
fly. (v)
follow
food
foot[ball]
for
foreign
fork
forward

free
friend
from
front
full
funny
furniture

game
garage
garden
gas
gate
gentleman
get
girl
give
glass
glue
go
goal
good (better, best)
goodbye
gramophone
grand- (e.g. in
    grandfater)
green
grey
ground
group
guest
gun

hair
half
hall
hammer
hand
handkerchief
happy
hard
hat
hate
have
he
head
headmaster/
heavy
here

65

hide (v) ladder meal nil
high lady measure no
history lake meat none
hit lamp meet north
hobby land mend nose
hold language metre not
hole last midday now
holiday late middle number
home[work] laugh midnight nurse
hook lavatory milk
horse lazy minute (n.)
hospital leaf Miss o'clock
host[ess] leave miss (n.) of
hot left mistake off
hotel leg mistress office
hour less model officer
house lesson money often
how letter monkey old
hungry lid month on
hurt lie (v) moon once
husband light (a.) more one (and -one e.g.
light (n. and v) morning in anyone)
like (a.) most open
I like (v) mother or
ice-cream line mountain orange
ill lion mouse other
in[to] listen moustache out
ink little mouth over
iron live (n.) Mr[s]
island living-room much
it loaf mud[dy] page
lock[ed] music paper
long (a. and n.) parcel
jam look parent
jar lose nail pass
journey lot name passenger
jug loud narrow past
jump love nasty pen
luggage near pencil
lump needle penny
key lunch neighbour people
kick neither person
kill nephew photograph
kilo[gram] magazine net picnic
kilometre make never picture
kind (a.) man new piece
kitchen many newspaper pillow
kite map next plate
knife marbles nice play[ground]
knock mat niece p.m.
match night pocket

policeman
pool (*e.g.*
   swimming-pool)
poor
port
post[card]
pot
pound
prefer
present (*a.*)
pretty
pull
pupil
push
put

quarter
quick
quiet
quite

radio
rain[y]
rat
rather
reach
read
red
rich
ride
right
ring (*n.*)
ring (*v*)
river
road
roof
room
rope
round
row (*v*)
rubber
rug
ruler
run

sail
salt
same

save
say
school
scissors
score
sea
seat
second (*n.*)
see
seldom
-self/selves
sell
send
servant
several
sew
shallow
shape
she
sheep
sheet
shelf
shine
ship
shirt
shoe
shoot
shop
short
shout
side
since
sing[er]
sister
sit
size
skirt
sky
sleep[y]
slice
slow
small
smile
smoke
snake
snow
soap
sock
soft
soldier
some

sometimes
son
song
south
speak
spoon[ful]
spring (*n.*)
square
stairs (*also* -stairs,
   e.g. in upstairs)
stamp
stand
star
station
stay
steal
stick (*n.*)
sticky
stocking
stone
stop
storm[y]
stove
straight
street
string
strong
student
study
stupid
such
sugar
sum
summer
sun[ny]
sweep
sweet
swim
sword

table
tail
take
talk
tall
tank
tap
tea
teach[er]
team

telephone
tennis
tent
than
that/those
the
theatre
then
there
they
thick
thief
thin
thing (*also* -thing,
   e.g. in nothing)
thirsty
this/these
through
throw
ticket
tie
tiger
time
tin
tired
to
today
together
tomorrow
tonight
too
tooth
top
towards
towel
tower
town
toy
train (*n.*)
tree
trip
trousers
truck
turn
twice
type (*v*)
typist

ugly
umbrella

67

uncle	wall	when	wood
under	want	where (*also*	word
university	warm	-where, *e.g. in*	work
up	wash	nowhere)	world
usually	watch (*n.*)	which	write
	water	white	wrong
	way	who	
van	we	why	
vayage	weak	wide	
very	wear	wife	year
village	weather	win	yellow
visit[or]	week	wind[y]	yes
volley-ball	weigh	window	yesterday
	well (*a.*)	winter	you
	west	wipe	young
wait	wet	wire	
wake	what	with[out]	
walk[ing-stick]	wheel	woman	zoo

Answer Key
Introductory Stories for Reproduction 2

STORY 1 *(p. 4)*

A.
1. Because she wanted a picture for her living-room.
2. A picture of a young girl.
3. 'How much do you want for this picture?'
4. 'Thirteen pounds.'
5. 'Thirty pounds? That's very expensive. I'm going to offer you twenty pounds for it.'

B. 1. expensive 2. back 3. more 4. much 5. few 6. young

C. 2, 7, 4, 8, 6, 3, 5, 1

STORY 2 *(p. 6)*

A.
1. Foreign food.
2. To a new Greek restaurant.
3. A button.
4. 'Look here, waiter! I've found this button in my food.'
5. 'Thank you, thank you! I looked everywhere for it.'

B. 1a, 2c, 3b, 4a, 5b

C. name, city, restaurant, waiter, lunch, food, eating, newspaper, office

STORY 3 *(p. 8)*

A.
1. To a circus.
2. She put a cake in her mouth.
3. It took the cake out of the beautiful girl's .mouth.
4. 'Who's going to do the same for £100?'
5. 'All right ... but first take the lion away!'

B. 1. first 2. people 3. shouted 4. next 5. beautiful

C. 1a, 2b, 3a, 4b, 5b, 6b

STORY 4 *(p.10)*

A.
1. 'It's a beautiful day, and it's hot in town. I'm going to drive out into the country and have a picnic in a quiet field there.'

2. A small country road.
3. 'This road's very steep, isn't it?'
4. 'Is this road dangerous?'
5. 'No, it isn't dangerous up here. They always crash down at the bottom.'

B. 1. in 2. on 3. in 4. on 5. at 6. in 7. at 8. at

C. dangerously, dangerous, slowly, quiet, quietly, beautiful, beautifully

STORY 5 (*p. 12*)

A. 1. Fishing.
2. To Scotland.
3. They fished.
4. To her neighbour, Mrs. Andrews.
5. She talked loudly in the boat, she put the wrong things on her hook, she pulled her line in very quickly, and she caught a lot more fish than her husband did.

B. 1, 4, 5, 8, 10

C. trousers, bag, basket, boat, beach, water, rowed, island, fly, hook

STORY 6 (*p. 14*)

A. 1. 'I'm not going to find nice, fresh fish in the London shops. They lie there for days and weeks.'
2. In a fish shop near her house.
3. She went into the shop and looked at all the fish there.
4. 'These ones aren't fresh. Look at them!'
5. 'That's your fault, not mine. These same fish were here in this shop last Friday, but you didn't buy them then, did you?'

B.

C. 1d, 2a, 3e, 4b, 5c

STORY 7 *(p. 16)*

A. 1. He pulled her bad tooth out.
       2. 'Does it still hurt, Helen?'
       3. 'I don't know.'
       4. 'Why don't you know?'
       5. 'Because the dentist's got it.'

B. 1. take 2. later 3. bad 4. cried 5. afternoon 6. kindly 7. new
        8. began

C. 1, 4, 2, 3, 6, 8, 5, 7

STORY 8 *(p. 18)*

A. 1. Because she had five children.
       2. A notice.
       3. 'I do cleaning for £1.50 an hour. Telephone Miss Joan Brown,
          7508.'
       4. 'Nobody's looking. That's good.'
       5. 'I do cleaning for nothing. Don't telephone me!'

B. 1b, 2b, 3b, 4a, 5a

C. shops, carpet, plates, pot, lid, broken, ring, cross, camera, films

STORY 9 *(p. 20)*

A. 1. In hot, sunny countries.
       2. 'I'm going to put some of my tables in the street here too.'
       3. He went to Renato's restaurant.
       4. It rained all the time.
       5. Because the rain fell into his plate.

B. 1. usually 2. fresh 3. people 4. lunch 5. most

C. 1a, 2b, 3b, 4a, 5b, 6a

STORY 10 *(p. 22)*

A. 1. It stopped.
       2. He got out, opened the bonnet and looked at the engine.
       3. He ran to the car and began pulling one of the red lights off the
          back of it.
       4. 'What are you doing there?'
       5. 'You can steal the pieces at the front. I'm going to take the ones
          at the back.'

B. 1. a few 2. a little 3. a few 4. a little 5. a little 6. a few
7. a little 8. a few

C. 1. doing 2. making, made, do 3. making, make 4. doing, doing

STORY 11 (*p. 24*)

A. 1. Because he got up very early.
2. Because his aeroplane to New York was very early.
3. George did.
4. Photographs of Mr. and Mrs. Andrews.
5. 'That's very good. I'm not going to eat my breakfast alone this morning.'

B. 2, 3, 6, 8, 9

C. Tower, Bridge, theatre, cinema, zoo, factory, football, map, policemen, soldiers

STORY 12 (*p. 26*)

A. 1. 'Your father always sold me good coal. There was never much dust in the sacks.'
2. 'I do that too.'
3. He brought Mrs. Black another two sacks of coal.
4. 'Did you find any dust in the last sacks of coal?'
5. 'No, I didn't find any *dust* in the sacks of *coal.* I found some pieces of *coal* in the sacks of *dust.*'

B.

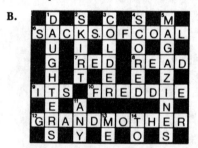

C. 1b, 2a, 3d, 4c

— 72 —

STORY 13 (*p. 28*)

A.   1. A poor man.
      2. He said, 'Good morning,' and gave the man 20p.
      3. No.
      4. Because he did not smoke.
      5. 'Sir, the matches cost 25p now!'

B.   1. sold 2. take 3. always 4. day 5. poor 6. shouted 7. fast
      8. narrow

C.   6, 3, 5, 8, 4, 2, 7, 1

STORY 14 (*p. 30*)

A.   1. His Uncle Fred.
      2. Neil showed his uncle his toys, and they talked for half an hour.
      3. 'I'm going to go out and play with God in the garden now.'
      4. 'How do you play with God?'
      5. 'It's easy. I throw the ball up, and then God throws it back
         down to me.'

B.   1b, 2c, 3a, 4a, 5b

C.   parents, house, country, neighbours, play, dishes, kitchen, toys,
      garden, throw

STORY 15 (*p. 32*)

A.   1. They got into their police car at the police station and drove
         around from eight o'clock to midnight.
      2. A few drunk people.
      3. 'Look, Jack. That man's going round and round a tree, and he's
         knocking at it all the time.'
      4. 'Go home.'
      5. 'Don't be stupid. There's a wall right round me.'

B.   1. around 2. first 3. home 4. midnight 5. together

C.   1b, 2c, 3a, 4b, 5c, 6a

STORY 16 (*p. 34*)

A.   1. They both worked hard in a shop.
      2. A big, new stereo.
      3. One of their neighbours.
      4. 'We've got a beautiful, new stereo now. Come to our flat and

listen to it this evening.'

5. 'No, come to our flat and listen to it there.'

B. 1. We 2. our 3. ours 4. us 5. you 6. yours, your

C. music, radio, stereo, singers, wife, artist, pictures, models, camera, photograph

STORY 17 (*p. 36*)

A. 1. He was George's friend.

2. George did not do much work, but Peter worked very hard.

3. He stood at one of the windows of the office.

4. 'There's a very lazy man in the street in front of the office. He began digging a hole this morning, but he hasn't done any work for half an hour.'

5. The man in the street and George.

B. 1, 4, 5, 8, 10

C. Neither, both, all, None, all, none

STORY 18 (*p. 38*)

A. 1. 'What are you going to eat, Susan?'

2. 'Those fish look good, don't they?

3. 'Yes, they do. I know a lot about fish.'

4. 'These fish are French, aren't they?'

5. 'I don't know. They haven't spoken to me.'

B.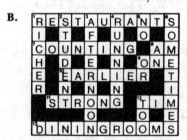

C. 1e, 2a, 3d, 4b, 5c

STORY 19 (*p. 40*)

A. 1. Because it was a very hot day in the middle of summer, and there were no trees along the street.

2. A small boy.

3. He followed Mr. Brown. He stayed very near him all the time, and he kicked the heels of Mr. Brown's shoes several times.
4. 'What are you doing? Stop following me like that! You're going to hurt my heels.'
5. 'Please don't stop me! It's very hot today, and there isn't any shade anywhere else in the street!'

B. 1. hot 2. near 3. small 4. fat 5. shade 6. summer

C. 6, 5, 8, 2, 1, 3, 4, 7

STORY 20 (*p. 42*)

A. 1. He had lessons.
    2. A good skydiver.
    3. 'How do you jump out of an aeroplane like that?'
    4. 'It's going to crash in a few seconds.'
    5. He jumps out quickly, because he is very afraid.

B. 1b, 2a, 3c, 4a

C. aeroplanes, expensive, flying, air, crash, club, lessons, afraid, brave, Jump

STORY 21 (*p. 44*)

A. 1. 'Aunt Kathy and Aunt Judy are going to visit us tomorrow. They live in Canada, and you haven't met them, because they very seldom come to England. They're going to have lunch with us.'
    2. At twelve o'clock the next day.
    3. Some coffee.
    4. 'She isn't very p-r-e-t-t-y, is she?'
    5. 'No, but I'm very c-l-e-v-e-r.'

B. 1. pretty 2. clever 3. visit 4. loved 5. aunt

C. 1b, 2a, 3b, 4b, 5a

STORY 22 (*p. 46*)

A. 1. It went through her coat.
    2. 'I want a good coat for my walks. I'm going to go to the shops tomorrow, and I'm going to buy one.'
    3. She went into a shop and looked at some coats with the salesgirl.
    4. 'This seal coat's nice, but does the rain come through it?'
    5. 'Have you ever seen a seal with an umbrella?'

B. 1. is driving, drives 2. is putting, puts 3. is going, goes

C. thin, fat, clothes, put, angry, said, dance, club, went, sizes

STORY 23 (*p. 48*)

A. 1. He gave him a piece of paper and said, 'Write your answers under the questions.'
   2. 'Have you ever been in prison?'
   3. 'No.'
   4. 'Why?'
   5. 'Because the police have never caught me.'

B. 2, 4, 5, 7, 10

C. 1. In A, Ted is wearing a dark cap. In B, he is wearing a white one.
   2. In A, four people are waiting. In B, two people are waiting.
   3. In A, it is raining. In B, the sun is shining.

STORY 24 (*p. 50*)

A. 1. 'I've got some work in Boxbury. Come with me and do your shopping there.'
   2. Because her husband very seldom took her out, and she usually shopped in their small village.
   3. To the River Dee.
   4. 'A pound for the car and twenty-five pence for the passenger.'
   5. 'Take the car for a pound, but I'm not going to sell my wife for less than fifty pence.'

B.

C. 1e, 2d, 3c, 4b, 5a

STORY 25 (*p. 52*)

A. 1. Sweets.

2. They looked into the window of the shop, and put their fingers on the glass.
3. 'Children! Do not put your fingers on this glass! It is dangerous!'
4. 'Why is the glass in your shop dangerous? What does it do to the children?'
5. 'The glass doesn't do anything to the children, but *I* give them a hard smack.'

B. 1. after 2. dirty 3. into 4. answer 5. left 6. hard 7. give
8. beautiful

C. 4, 6, 5, 7, 2, 1, 8, 3

STORY 26 (*p. 54*)

A. 1. 'Who's there?' 'William, Captain.'
2. 'What are you doing there, William?' 'Nothing, Captain.'
3. 'Is Tom there?' 'Yes, he is.'
4. 'What's he doing?'
5. 'He's helping me, Captain.'

B. 1c, 2a, 3a, 4b, 5a

C. captain, ship, engines, port, lazy, work, busy, stairs, helping, empty

STORY 27 (*p. 56*)

A. 1. He lost them.
2. 'Umbrellas are expensive, David, and you buy one every week. Bring this one home this evening.'
3. An umbrella.
4. He said, 'Today I'm not going to lose my umbrella,' and he took it, got out of the train at his station and brought the umbrella home.
5. 'But, David, you didn't take an umbrella with you this morning. That one isn't yours!'

B. 1. evening 2. expensive 3. every 4. often 5. home

C. 1a, 2b, 3b, 4a, 5a, 6b

STORY 28 (*p. 58*)

A. 1. Because he did not have much money.
2. In the dining-room of the hotel.
3. A plate.

4. 'Waitress, this plate's wet.'
5. 'That's your soup.'

B. 1. a 2. The, the, the 3. The, the, the, a 4. The, a 5. The 6. a 7. an
8. The 9. the a 10, The, the

C. hotel, bar, bath, lavatory, basin, bed, chicken, duck.

STORY 29 (*p. 60*)

A. 1. 'I want a cat, Mummy.'
2. From a neighbour.
3. He pulled its tail.
4. 'Don't pull the kitten's tail, Jack.'
5. 'I'm not pulling it, Mummy. I'm holding it, and the kitten's
pulling.'

B. 2, 3, 6, 8

C. 1a. Whose 1b. What 1c. Why 2a. What 2b. Who 2c. What
3a. Where 3b. How 3c. Which

STORY 30 (*p. 62*)

A. 1. Because it was higher.
2. 'Please come and sit in my truck.'
3. They went and sat in the truck.
4. Because it was heavy.
5. 'Now all of us are friends!'

B.

C. 1c, 2d, 3e, 4b, 5a

저자소개

L. A. Hill 박사는 ELT (English Language Teaching)
교재의 저술가로서 그리고 영어 교육계의 세계적인
권위자로 널리 알려진 분으로 그의 저서에는 다음과 같은
것들이 있다.
Stories for Reproduction 1 (전 4 권), Stories for
Reproduction 2 (전 4 권), Stories for Reproduction:
American Series (전 3 권), Steps to Understanding
(전 4 권), Word Power 1500/3000/4500 (전 3 권),
English through Cartoons (전 2 권), Elementary &
Intermediate Composition Pieces (전 2 권), Elementary &
Intermediate Comprehension Pieces (전 2 권),
Intermediate Comprehension Topics, Oxford Graded
Readers (전 4 권), Writing for a Purpose, Note-taking
Practice, A Guide to Correct English & Exercises
(전 2 권), Prepositions & Adverbial Particles &
Exercises (전 2 권), Contextualized Vocabulary Tests
(전 4 권), Crossword Puzzle Book (전 4 권).

Introductory Stories for Reproduction 2

1985년 2 월 5 일 인쇄
1985년 2 월 12일 발행

지은이   L. A. HILL
펴낸이   李 瀅 載
펴낸곳   外國語研修社

판권
본사   소유

서울·영등포구 여의도동 35-2
등록   1977. 5 . 18. 제10-81호
전화   785-0919, 1749

판 매 가 격
8000

Oxford 대학출판부/외국어연수사간(한국내 판권 : 외국어연수사에서 보유)
ESL/EFL 교재 저술의 세계적 권위 L.H.Hill박사의 명저

Stories for Reproduction Series 1~4

이야기의 재현(再現)을 통해 배우는 영어1~4집

■흥미진진한 이야기를 읽거나 듣고 말과 글로 다시 표현해 보는 연습을 통해 표현력(作文·會話)·이해력(讀解·聽解)을 획기적으로 향상시키는 교재

● 이미 40여권의 ESL/EFL(English as a Second/Foreign Language) 교재 저술로 세계적 명성을 떨치고 있는 Leslie A. Hill 박사가 그의 오랜 연구와 교육자로서의 경험을 토대로 최근에 집대성한 영어학습교재의 결정판.

● Hill박사 특유의 Contextualized Approach(문맥적 접근법)에 토대를 둔 다양한 Oral/Written Reproduction Questions & Exercises(구두/필기재현연습)로 표현력과 이해력의 획기적 향상.

● A. S. Hornby 의 Guide to Patterns & Usage in English(25 구문 유형)에 토대를 두고 단어와 구문의 난이도에 따라 상용 기본단어를 4 단계(입문, 초급, 중급, 상급)로 나누어 익히고 활용시키는 교재 총서.

● 영어 실력이 약한 경우는 기초실력 재확립용으로, 어휘력·문법실력이 앞선 경우는 속독력·청해력·작문력·회화력 향상용으로 쓸 수 있는 교재.

● 교실수업, 자습 양용으로 쓸 수 있으며 자습의 경우를 위해 상세하고 친절한 주석과 해답이 담긴 Study Guide와 Answer Key를 마련.

■대학입시·취직시험·각종고시·TOFEL 등 각종 영어 시험 준비용으로 최적.

제 1 집 Introductory, Elementary, Intermediate Advanced Stories for Reproduction 1
전 4권 Textbook+Study Guide+Cassette Pack.

제 2 집 Introductory, Elementary, Intermediate, Advanced Stories for Reproduction 2
전 4권 Textbook+Answer Key+Cassette Pack.

제 3 집 Introductory, Elementary, Intermediate, Advanced Steps to Understanding
전 4권 Textbook+Answer Key+Cassette Pack.

제 4 집 Elementary, Intermediate, Advanced Stories for Reproduction, American
Series 전 3권 Textbook+Answer Key+Cassette Pack.

영어단어연습문제 및 해답 각 3권
Word Power 1500/3000/4500 (한국판)
Vocabulary Tests & Exercises in American English

한국내 정가 각권당 : 문제집 ₩ 2,000 ; 해답집 ₩ 500

■EFL/ESL (English as a Foreign/Second Language) 교사 및 저술가로서 세계적 권위 Leslie A. Hill 박사의 최신의 명저.

■문맥적 시험 및 연습(Contextualized Tests & Exercises)을 통한 어휘·작문·독해·회화 실력의 동시 양성.

■대입고사·취직시험·각종 고시·TOEFL 등 각종 시험 준비에 최적

●Structure Words의 철저한 시험/연습으로 구문력(構文力) 양성.

●Picture/Passage의 문맥적 연습(단어의 문맥적 추리→해답과 대조→기억→활용) 으로 독해력(讀解力) 향상.

●Synonyms(유어), Oppoites(반의어), Derivatives(파생어) 의 연습으로 풍부한 표현력 (작문력, 회화력) 양성.

●Words in Sentences 연습으로 Content Words 및 Structure Words의 활용 능력 향상

●Prepositions 및 Adverbial Particles(구동사 : 句動詞) 연습으로 미국 영어 숙어 (熟 語) 의 정확한 용법 체득.

Executive English
경영자의 영어
Philip Binham 著 李瀅載 訳註

음성교재 : 카셋트 테이프 C60×9개 정가 : 교재 권당 ₩ 3,000 테이프 권당3개 : ₩ 15,000

■독해←→작문←→대화·연습을 상호 연관적으로 연수시켜 높은 수준의 영어 구사력 양성.

■경영의 모든 분야에서 실용되는 보고서, 문서, 서신, 대화, 연설, 국제회의 등을 총 망라한 종합 실용 영어.

■고졸 수준이면 쉽게 공부할 수 있도록 영한 대역, 단어·숙어·용법등에 대한 상세한 영영한 주해 및 예문을 수록.

■Longman의 Master Tape로 제작된 최고 음질의 음성교재.

Oxford대학출판부·외국어연수사간

만화를 즐기며 연마하는 영어 회화 · 작문교재

전 2 권

English through Cartoons

Dialogues, Stories & Questions

Book 1 ~ 2

한국내판권보유 : 외국어연수사

유우머와 기지가 넘치는 만화를 즐기면서

(A) 대화(Dialogues)를 읽거나 테이프를 듣고 영어 특유의
　　유우머 감각을 몸에 익히며

(B) 만화를 해설하는 이야기 (Stories)를 공란을 메우면서 완성하는
　　연습을 통해 작문력을 기르고

(C) 만화내용의 질의 응답을 통해 격조 높은 영어 회화력을
　　양성하는 영작문 · 회화 연습 교재의 결정판 /

● EFL/ESL (English as a Foreign/Second Language) 교재 저술의 세계적 권위
　Leslie A. Hill 박사와 세계적인 만화가 D. Mallet 의 최신 역작.

● 폭소와 홍소를 자아내게 하면서도 깊은 뜻을 담은 만화와 대화는 학습상의 긴장을
　덜어 주며 Stories 의 공란을 추리하여 완성토록 유도하는 연습문제와 내용 파악
　질의문은 영어의 회화력·청취력·작문력·독해력을 획기적으로 연마·향상.

● 학습 부담을 줄이고 능률을 최대한으로 올리기 위하여 친절하고 자세한 해설과 예문이
　풍부하게 수록된 Study Guide 를 따로 마련.